EPITAPHS
FOR THE PLAGUE DEAD

Robert Boucheron

URSUS PRESS
New York
1985

Library of Congress Catalog Card Number: 85-51479

ISBN: 0-9615441-0-4

Ursus Press, P.O. Box 1261, Old Chelsea Station, New York, NY 10113.

 Produced at The Print Center., Inc., 225 Varick St., New York, NY 10014, a non-profit facility for literary and arts-related publications. (212) 206-8465

Preface

As I write in the summer of 1985, our medical knowledge of AIDS is far from perfect. There is no diagnostic test for the disease, no positive identification of the cause (although a virus seems most likely), no hope of a cure, and no end in sight. Even narrowly defined, the reported caseload continues to double every six months, so the federal government has declared an epidemic. The alarming symptoms and high mortality of AIDS, as well as the social cruelty it provokes, allow us to call it a plague.

AIDS has attacked people regardless of sex and personal behavior. But in the United States, the greatest number of sufferers are male and homosexual, and those who have died have often been young. Because some Americans see this pattern as a divine judgment, the disease has become another test of our identity, of our collective spirit. In more than one sense, we are fighting for our lives.

As part of our struggle for understanding, then, both among ourselves and in the world at large, I offer these fictional epitaphs, which focus on the problems and personalities of gay men. But within this focus, I have tried to draw subjects from all walks of life, with varying degrees of self-knowledge, and speaking in their own voices. In some cases, I have used the words we actually say, with all their latent confusion. Some of the subjects are based on real individuals, but none entirely so. Each attempts to depict a type of man or an aspect of the tragedy.

The device of having each man speak for himself is certainly not new. The *Greek Anthology* contains fictional epitaphs from before the time of Christ. These have inspired others, notably those in Edgar Lee Masters's *Spoon River Anthology* and Thornton Wilder's *Our Town*. And A. E. Housman's *A Shropshire Lad* impresses me as an attempt to give contemporary life a classical weight and tone.

As for the rhymed, metrical form, it simply appeared with the first poems. It turned out, of course, to be the stanza of *In Memoriam*, by Tennyson. I believe this reference is apt, since Tennyson's poem sequence deals with his grief for Arthur Hallam, a young man to whom the poet was strongly attached. While I do not claim to have emulated the beauty of Tennyson's language, I hope I have given these voices form and dignity, and a grace that belongs not to real life, but to art.

The matter of Tennyson's verse appeals to us less strongly than it did to the Victorians. But I wish to quote the last stanza of his "Prologue" as oddly relevant to the work in hand, allowing for a pun in the phrase "wasted youth," and shifting the address to you, the reader:

> Forgive these wild and wandering cries,
>   Confusions of a wasted youth;
>   Forgive them where they fail in truth,
> And in thy wisdom make me wise.

Contents

EPITAPHS FOR THE PLAGUE DEAD

Epitaph for a Front Runner

Leading the avant-garde for once,
I who could barely keep abreast
of fashion here am laid to rest,
for lack of an immune response,

which seems ironic, since I styled
my ready answers with a quote
from some gay personage of note,
a quip worthy of Oscar Wilde.

New to the scene, I did what pleases,
danced all night at exclusive clubs,
drank in the bars, soaked in the tubs,
and caught a number of diseases.

Upwardly mobile, affluent,
I carelessly shrugged off the cost
of medicine and workdays lost,
and thought my innocence well-spent,

though Fire Island rentals nearly
emptied me of my last few cents,
after the co-op maintenance,
and all the drugs we loved so dearly,

along with Calvin, Ralph, and Bill,
and membership at the right gym
to keep my body sleek and slim,
and therapy for a thin will.

But even so, I lagged behind
the favored few who set the pace.
Life on the circuit was some race,
headed to what, I paid no mind,

until I caught a plague so new
the doctors only diagnosed
it just as I gave up the ghost,
unconscious of my final coup.

Epitaph for an Artist

Once mentioned as a promising
young artist for my bold technique,
my grasp of discipline was weak:
I finished hardly anything.

My specialty was portrait heads
of lovers, friends, acquaintances,
a businessman who paid for his,
well-groomed models, and unmade beds.

I loved to paint youth's larval stage,
the pretty blankness like a blur,
or etch the lines of character,
frank or reserved, that comes with age.

Life-size or larger, I would paint
them streaming clouds of colored fire,
the nimbus that all lives inspire,
seen in the halo of a saint.

But while my hand sketched pain and bliss
on the raw canvas of sex, it shivered,
and failed before my art delivered,
and so my promise came to this.

Epitaph for an Officer

A year of mourning was the norm
perhaps a century ago
for next of kin, but even so,
you might take off that uniform.

Going in drag was not our style,
but since I left the service late,
I took you as my second mate,
willing to ship aboard on trial.

We sailed some fifteen years together,
and over all our course blew fair.
One more you added to our share,
although the last was heavy weather.

But even after all this time,
I hear you whimpering alone,
afraid to sail out on your own,
rotting at anchor in your prime.

You always needed a big shove,
but underway you spring no leaks.
So now hear this, your captain speaks:
cast off and ease away, my love.

Epitaph for a Bodybuilder

A body that went on for days
was what I had, a torrid torso,
with arms and shoulders even more so,
and a tight butt that garnered praise

in competitions coast to coast.
I won the Mr. Wonder title,
which got my photograph and vital
stats in the mags that matter most.

With iron in my hands and diet,
I made myself a work of art,
as near perfect in every part
as man can be, no way to buy it.

The guys were all hot to connect,
and so was I, but on the side —
one-night affairs. I always tried
to keep a healthy self-respect.

Somehow I caught the dreaded bug,
and as my mighty muscles shrank,
I wondered who in hell to thank,
until I gave up with a shrug.

Epitaph for a Hick

Back home, when all my chores were done,
I whistled up old Jack and took
a rod and headed out the brook
to hike and fish in the late sun.

Ma, she was quiet, let me find
my own way, even when it led
to streets and bright lights, though she said
my heart was like to stay behind.

A job just fell on top of me:
two callused hands and a strong back
are all you really need to stack
machine parts in a factory.

I worked hard, like a country hick,
and found a place to eat and sleep,
not much to brag about, but cheap,
and I was happy as a tick.

I thought I went to paradise,
the people downtown dressed so well.
The men especially looked swell,
like angels, with a secret vice.

I picked up that one, I confess,
in two shakes of a new lamb's tail.
The eyes of love could then unveil
their tricks and know true loneliness.

But I was hooked on the barbed bait
in more ways than I knew at first,
and though I prayed to God and cursed,
by that time it was too damned late.

7

Epitaph for an Islander

I never drank the island rum,
or walked the land I fertilize,
or saw it with my own two eyes,
but this is still where I was from.

And though I never learned to speak in
Spanish except to deal and swear,
my dark brown skin and straight black hair
and broad face made me Puerto Rican.

For some it was an insult, pure
and simple: others thought I must
be sensual and filled with lust,
born to a higher temperature.

They all assumed that I would fuck
sooner than eat, hung like a horse,
that I would eat like one or worse,
and steal them blind with any luck.

No animal, I left that pack.
My family picked out a wife,
but witnessing my burned-out life,
took care of me and brought me back.

Epitaph for an Older Man

An older man, I called myself
a sexy senior citizen,
a hot sexagenarian,
not one to molder on the shelf.

I never lost my taste for meat,
and packers were surprised to sense
the depth of my experience:
I took my dentures out to eat.

Nor did I lose my boyish charm,
my lanky adolescent figure,
my wavy hair, or manly vigor,
thanks to growing up on the farm.

Exceptionally well-maintained,
I outstripped men of half my years,
youngsters still wet behind the ears,
gasping for breath — but none complained.

Age is supposed to be mature,
but I stayed giddy till the end,
blissfully ignorant, my friend,
that this gay life might not endure.

Epitaph for an Achiever

Given to lists, the future tense,
and hard work, not just getting by,
I set my goals and standards high
and kept a scrapbook of events.

Affection for another man
could not affect my rise, I knew.
Death at the age of thirty-two
formed no part of my long range plan.

Epitaph for a Patient

The smell was what I minded most,
although the rest was bad enough,
the constant heartburn, the dry cough,
fever, and all the weight I lost.

No part of me was not in pain,
from hands that swelled to football size
from I.V. tubes, to burning eyes,
to bowels that ran and ran in vain.

The gaudy skin tones, and a host
of purple bumps were hard to take,
but breathing on my own, awake,
the smell was what I minded most.

Epitaph for a Physician

Hardly one of your backstreet thugs,
I built up quite a practice in
basic internal medicine,
which helped support my taste for drugs.

I started during internship
to get me through the blood and stink
and double shifts without a wink:
the stuff was there, and I was hip.

The pressure never really eased.
I got in deeper, even stole
dispensary supplies. Control
was needle-slender, and I squeezed.

My friends and patients, mostly gay,
thought drugs were recreational.
As a physician, I could call
the shots and did, for work and play.

The pills and poppers magnified
the good times and the risks as well,
said someone trying to raise hell,
but that was social suicide.

Epitaph for a Whiz Kid

Debate team champ at Bishop Tuttle,
I judged myself as pretty smart.
I thought fast on my feet to start,
then crushed the bastards in rebuttal.

Good college, made the law review,
a Wall Street firm in litigation.
Slick in a sticky situation,
no loophole I could not squeeze through.

My arguments were late-night news,
delivered like a contact sport.
I knocked them out in civil court,
shaking in their expensive shoes.

My estimate went up a notch
each time I scored another punch.
Singled out at a partners' lunch,
I knew I was the one to watch.

No dizzy barflies for this ace:
I cruised to win and got my fill
of rearguard action up until
I lost my first and biggest case.

Epitaph for a Suicide

From Faulkner country and a clan
to rival his most Gothic fable,
I was declared to be unstable,
which subsequently served my plan.

For when the fateful news came through
assigning me the worst of ills,
I staged an accident with pills,
which only verified their view.

Epitaph for a Drag Queen

My obsequies were numerous,
the private chapel was refined,
and darling, you could hardly find
my casket for the floral cross.

I only wish, for all the girls —
and almost everyone was there —
that Mama would have let me wear
my pink dress with the cultured pearls.

My wayward ways brought her no joy:
she said it was unnatural
to act up like some nigger gal,
when I was such a nice black boy.

What did she know to criticize?
Searching for glamor, style, and chic,
I combed the Gay Paree Boutique
for something tasteful in my size.

Of course, with what I had to choose,
my outfits may have been outdated,
but never uncoordinated —
I owned a dozen pairs of shoes.

And no one could accessorize
as I did, the right hat and bag.
Those who saw but a queen in drag
had mortal scales before their eyes.

The undertaker had to sell
a blue serge suit, my deepest fear,
then close the lid. But frankly, dear,
I was not looking all that well.

Epitaph for a Success

I had a flair for sell and buy sense,
so when my thespian career
did not pan out, I shifted gear
and wound up with a broker's license.

I ran my own consulting firm
for new investors, and increased
my worth twelvefold, or ten at least,
all safely sheltered and long-term.

I filled my renovated space
with giant plants, just like a green-
house, furniture all European,
with tracks on dimmers everyplace.

I had it all except one thing,
a lover who could share my dream,
but though I entertained the cream,
I never saw it happening.

Epitaph for a Failure

As you go forth alive and free,
in hot pursuit of happiness,
consider what a sorry mess
I made, and stop, and pity me.

Epitaph for a Dealer

Throwing off sparks and flying high,
I took the fast lane all the way,
and did a fat, white line a day,
and knew that I would never die.

Napoleon once said it best:
"The bullet that will bring me down
has not been cast." All over town,
I felt on top of Everest.

They called me Frosty the Snow Queen,
an entertainment catalyst,
a must on any party list,
the gay man's good times go-between.

But once, vacuuming up the rows
on someone's glass-topped writing desk,
my face in close-up looked grotesque,
a rolled twenty stuck up my nose.

My final stop turned out to be
no bullet, but a slow decline.
So babe, I lay you one last line:
high living was the death of me.

Epitaph for a Victim

A head too big for what was left,
a sack of soup bones for a body,
I watched TV all day on shoddy
cushions I could no longer heft.

It takes two orderlies to pull
me up the stairs, and then they scram.
A handmade sign nailed to the jamb:
"Keep Away—Danger," and a skull.

The landlord walks away. The place
has violations up the butt,
with windows smashed or painted shut.
No rent to pay, the saving grace.

Of all my so-called friends, not one
comes up to see me once they hear.
Food came thanks to a volunteer,
who took me down when it was done.

Epitaph for a Radical Fairy

Around the time the white man's "boy"
rose up in black anger and burned
the inner cities, and we learned
about the bombing of Hanoi,

the Pentagon's mass-murder trip,
incredibly done with consent
of Congress and the President,
the mind-war-game just made me flip.

Fresh out of jail, I turned my back
on the straight world of three-piece suits,
two-car garages, one-way routes,
and ground-zero missile attack,

to live in peace and fellow-feeling
among the vegetables and fruits,
and let my own late-starting roots
grope their way to the source of healing.

I swore off meat, and let my hair
and beard grow long and unrestrained.
My clothes were cast-offs, patched and stained,
and all I owned was free to share.

The neighbors viewed me with distrust
and thought I practiced magic arts,
a fantasy on both our parts:
I sprinkled them with fairy dust.

They granted that I made no noise,
lacking a tube or phonograph,
and rather liked my hearty laugh,
but warned away their little boys,

for fear that something terrible
might happen if they talked to me.
And so it would: the tykes might see
their parents' lives as so much bull.

Not for their eyes, I wrote and mailed
long poems to express the vibes
that unified the fairy tribes,
until the movement got derailed.

Done with discussing wrongs and rights,
I educated by example
and sang old hymn tunes in my ample
garden of heavenly delights.

Epitaph for a Proprietor

For daring young men, my trapeze
was famous, what with glory holes,
black leather, slave and master roles,
but basically the scene was sleaze.

After the first scare, business slipped,
so I installed a wash-up sink,
discouraged scat play for the stink,
kept tabs on who was really ripped,

sold condoms at the bar below,
and scrubbed the corners a little harder.
My place was clean and all in order:
the state grants licenses, you know.

The only raids I had at night
were when some queen not dressed to meet
the code got booted to the street
and called the cops out of pure spite.

No one got sick from taking part
in what my premises provided:
the issue here is many-sided.
Myself, I died of a weak heart.

Epitaph for a Patron

It must have been the slight skin rash,
who smiled so sweetly down the hall,
then propped his foot against the wall
to let his towel ride up and flash.

Or else it was the strong cologne,
who said he sweated quite a lot,
and certainly the room was hot,
and so was he, a tropic zone.

Or then there was the rasping cough,
who said that poppers gave him fits,
and wanted me to chew his tits
so hard I nearly bit them off.

Or once there was that swollen arm,
who overdid his workout press,
but exercised nevertheless
a cock quite capable of harm.

Or what about the fiery hole,
who lay in wait in the third booth,
face down and muttering uncouth
suggestions for a ten-foot pole?

Or could it be the bony frame,
whose metabolic rate was high,
who uttered that tremendous sigh
of pain or pleasure as he came?

The gummy mats, the fetid air,
the sauna, and the tile-faced ledge
had an uncomfortable edge
that kept me on the go while there,

and later in the testing lab,
where all the tricks came to be treated.
I felt a little used or cheated,
but hurried back upon rehab.

As deadly as they were sublime,
the tubs, though heaven for a spell,
turned out to be a steaming hell:
so many men, so little time.

Epitaph for an Atheist

God, I denied you in a clear
and strident voice to anyone
who listened in the street, and on
occasion to my own sole ear.

How can your goodness coexist
in all the evil that men do,
created likenesses of you
and so summarily dismissed?

Epitaph for a Forgiving Soul

Your will is done, Lord, and amen.
We all are sinners in your sight
and equally may claim the right
to pray to you as humble men.

Forgive the ignorance and fear
of those who preach your hand in this,
and let their hardened hearts not miss
the lesson they refuse to hear.

Epitaph for a Designer

Cut from common material,
I lived for clothes and by design,
making at least this title mine:
the best-dressed faggot of them all.

But for this body I did shape
a look, an outlook, and a kind
of beauty even, of the mind
more than of fine fabric and drape.

Some nights while working on my own,
time unravelled before my eyes
until the morning sun would rise,
and I would see my vision sewn.

Epitaph for a Hustler

Uncut, I had it where it counts,
what you might call the main attraction,
always up for a little action,
depositing in large amounts.

Chewing an unlit fag all day,
I worked the streets and sleazy bars
and learned to size them up by cars
or clothes, figuring what would pay.

Those first years I made out in style,
pulling them in while I was young.
Then I began to use my tongue —
for sweet talk: I was versatile.

I played for keeps, money or married,
what I could get. I was no fool,
screwing love in tight with my too!,
but all I got at last was buried.

21

Epitaph for a Disco Bunny

I ate to live but lived to dance
on weekends, any night I could,
at clubs whose sound was halfway good,
with almost anything in pants.

Amid the waving arms and screams,
I saw him sometimes, a cool head,
handsome and gentle, hot in bed,
the slow-dancing man of my dreams.

Epitaph for a Carrier

The thought that life might not proceed
much longer got me so uptight
and mad, especially at night,
that sex became a crying need.

Outwardly healthy, handsome still,
a little underweight perhaps,
I cruised the streets and tourist traps
and captured some of the old thrill.

Lately I filled the active slot.
My lesions were not visible,
but you could feel them up my hole.
I pulled out just before I shot.

Those tricks will never know how close
they came, but what the doctors said
might not be true, though I am dead.
What if a few more got the dose?

Epitaph for a Scholar

A scholar and a gentleman,
I carried off the Ivy look—
the rumpled blazer, pipe, and book—
with no sweat, and without a tan.

My dissertation on the diction
Whitman invented to invoke
his love of men was deemed a joke
in doubtful taste, like soft-core fiction.

I sought acknowledgment in schools
for homosexuality
in literary history,
which is to say, I broke the rules

and viva voce told the truth
about the brightest and the best.
Publishers' lack of interest
counted against me, as did youth.

Untenured, I was twice proposed,
but politics are Byzantine
throughout the academic scene,
and closet doors stay firmly closed.

Depressed, I courted suicide,
as have so many in our past,
harrowed by conscience and harassed,
unable to stand up with pride.

I overcame that ghost to bare
a post-war military scandal
the experts called too hot to handle,
but how much did they know or care?

The epidemic made this clear,
as publicly endowed research
threatened to leave us in the lurch,
under darkening clouds of fear.

Epitaph for an Intimate

Friend of the great, myself unknown,
invited to their smart to-dos,
I often was compelled to choose
whom to offend, how to atone.

Content to bask in their bright glory,
reflecting with my famous tact,
I found my niche. They knew I lacked
the drive that was their whole life-story.

This was the secret of their trust,
the key to cars, country retreats,
fabulous clothes, and theater seats,
until my polish showed some rust.

A famous actress then suggested
I skip the fall formalities
and winter somewhere in the Keys,
that is, until I felt more rested.

My sojourn in the hospital
lengthened to an extended stay,
but after the deluxe bouquet,
there came no further card or call.

Epitaph for a Motorcycle Priest

On Sundays, I roared up to Mass
in helmet, goggles, and astride
a big, black hog that squealed and shied,
as I turned sharp and cut the gas.

At St. Brendan's they called me Father
and little knew my daring search
for a full life outside the Church,
the back room bars, the hot and bother.

I served them as my talents suited,
but reinterpreted my vow
of strict chastity to allow
loving attachments, sex included.

I also kept my faith intact,
tempering narrow piety
with magic and astrology,
the basis of religious fact.

A psychiatric counsellor,
I lived and practiced in the city,
free of monastic rules and pity,
and in that setting never wore

the black shirt with the small white bit
right at the throat except to cheer
the Gay Pride rally once a year,
and hope the bishop had a fit.

That was a long way from the land
where I was born, an Irish lad,
expected to help feed and clad
my younger siblings, lend a hand

at chores all day, and bear the blame
for our endemic poverty.
An education was the key,
and I escaped, but not from shame.

For when I lay in torment, I
behaved no better than the least
of my poor parish, though a priest,
sweating, in tears, afraid to die.

Epitaph for a Dog Slave

Allow me, sir, to introduce
myself, an insolent young pup
who wanted to be left tied up,
a cur just asking for abuse.

In need of training, for a fact,
I carried my own leash and whip
and practiced how to whine and nip,
to get my tail end soundly smacked.

I liked a heavy guy, a bruiser,
a strict disciplinarian,
a ramrod military man
who pegged me for an all-time loser.

Down on my knees to beg for favor,
I licked his cruddy boots and feet.
Humiliation so complete
had an extraordinary flavor!

No lack of empathy could dim it,
and though I had a few close calls
with crazies out to bust my balls,
only here have I reached my limit.

Epitaph for a Bureaucrat

A lower level bureaucrat,
I shuffled documents and lives,
and filed away my deeper drives
to satisfy the fattest cat

in city hall. What could I do?
My boss, who shouted his dislikes,
made no secret of fags and dykes.
When I resigned, I think he knew.

Epitaph for a Trustee

Dark gray flannel down to my toes
suited me: banking was my bag.
Dressed for work in my midtown drag,
I supervised portfolios

of stocks and bonds in steel and oil,
all solid blue chip, held in trust
for children of the upper crust
with children of their own to spoil.

My modest salary sufficed
a man of modest aspiration.
I bought a co-op near the station,
a lower floor but underpriced.

A guest might try it on for size,
but mornings as a rule were brisk.
A bar is one thing, but to risk
your life's investment is unwise.

27

Epitaph for a Stammerer

A proposition made me stammer
and come across as touched or shy,
but I was just a clean-cut guy
with hands and arms like Arm & Hammer.

In school, they said my voice was good,
and songs came easy, so I let
the big talkers work up a sweat
and sang as often as I could.

Epitaph for a Teacher

Pencils clamped in their little fists,
their tongues stuck out in concentration,
my class took an examination
seriously, with no assists.

I loved to watch them come to grips
with concepts just beyond their reach.
Childless, my calling was to teach,
so call me a late Mr. Chips.

Like him, I see them always young,
bright as morning, and innocent.
My own night-shadowed life was spent
before its noontime bell had rung.

Epitaph for an Alcoholic

I told my story many times
at meetings, and I heard my share.
I learned a funny lesson there:
we love to advertise our crimes.

The trouble, like a dirty trick,
my family and friends went through,
and how many employers, too,
when I was drunk, now makes me sick.

Worst was the way my lover cared
and cleaned up from my late night wrecks.
The fights we had, and then the sex!
I guess we both were running scared.

At last he had enough of tears
and childish threats of suicide.
He kicked me out after I tried
to stab myself with pinking shears.

My life hit bottom as I made
one last attempt to drown my sorrow,
hoping there would be no tomorrow,
that night and I would simply fade.

From where I lay in my own spew,
a total stranger got me walking,
kept me from blacking out by talking,
and sponsored my AA debut.

It hurt like hell as I began
to grow at last and make amends,
but, with the endless help of friends,
I lived eight years a sober man.

Epitaph for a Collector

Born rich, I never had to hew
a path to what most people want.
I dabbled as a dilettante,
showing to a selected few.

A sensual aristocrat,
I cultivated modes and moods,
consumed the finest wines and foods,
and savored friends and friendly chat.

Into this life of perfect taste
death entered as something demeaning,
to say I lacked not means, but meaning:
now it all seems rather a waste.

Epitaph for an Aspiring Actor

I balanced plates and brimful glasses,
threaded my way through thick and thin,
took idle insults on the chin,
smiled a great deal, and turned down passes

from customers I waited on,
meanwhile rehearsing grief and rage,
faces and gestures for the stage,
waiting for my career to dawn.

I also cleaned apartment hallways,
walked dogs, scooped ice cream, drove a cab,
swung a hammer, and took a dab
at painting—with a roller, always.

A white flame burning in control,
one thing I had was energy.
Success would come: the world would see
that Homesick Sue was not my role.

Somehow I always paid the rent
and kept intact my sense of humor.
My big break came, but as a tumor
that broke my wick, and out I went.

Epitaph for a Sweet Tooth

Coming out, I felt like a kid
in candy stores that packed a sting,
gay bars that promised anything
might happen — and it often did.

A lifelong fan of M&M's,
and loyal to the one true brand,
I always kept a few on hand
to offer like sweet strategems.

Of course, with all the strain and stress
developed by a new romance,
they sometimes melted in my pants
and made an awful sticky mess.

But what really got me in trouble
was meeting someone for a date
way across town, and running late,
without my pack of Double Bubble.

I needed something that would last
to chew on while I danced, you know,
or when the music got too slow,
or I began to feel out-classed.

They say too many sweets will spoil
your appetite and rot your teeth.
I ate my fill and lie beneath
the dark and bitter-tasting soil.

Epitaph for an Innocent

I got it from my mother's breast,
unknowing, as an infant sips.
She got it from my father's lips,
conceiving in my interest.

He got it lying still in bed,
his arm connected to a sack
that, as a hemophiliac,
he needed any time he bled.

A small, unhappy family,
we shared more than a common cold.
For my part, the sum is soon told:
nine months I lived, dying in three.

Epitaph for a Sinner

I left the Baptist ministry
accused of moral turpitude,
of language that was low and lewd
and actions that were mighty free.

There was no trial, no chance to gawk:
the scandal would have rocked the state.
They hushed the papers, sealed my fate,
and watched those three boys like a hawk.

They stripped me of my ordination
and with it all my self-respect.
My car and my career were wrecked,
and I was driven to damnation.

I wandered with the mark of Cain
and tried to satiate my lust.
God knows my punishment was just,
to wallow in my precious bane.

At last a vagrant that police
told to move on, I stank of sin
and sank to begging coins, and in
my final weakness, I found peace.

Epitaph for a Minor Poet

The Fanny Cockburn Moody Prize
for Confidential Poetry,
worth fifty dollars, went to me
for my ambiguous disguise

of that affair with Reginald.
We were so young and steeped in Greek
mythology, and I was weak —
and then the bastard never called.

My posthumous revenge was decked
in rhyming octosyllables,
like pretty little pinkish pills
that sit awhile, then take effect.

My style was elegant and terse
and lilting as a summer swallow.
My imagery was hard to follow,
so they said, and a bit perverse.

My name appeared alongside those
of more established reputation.
Readers of some discrimination
might spot me sprinting through the rows

of Roman type in quarterlies,
matching pace with life to the letter.
I did well, but deserved much better,
numbered now with the rest of these.

Epitaph for a Shopgirl

Shopgirl, ribbon clerk, what you will,
or fairy, as my father said,
I felt no need to get ahead
or dip my fingers in the till.

My customers all got a smile,
the store owner an honest day.
Whose business could it be to say
my enterprise was not worthwhile?

Epitaph for a Chubbette

Not fat so much as overweight,
not overweight so much as plump,
well-padded in the hips and rump,
I had to watch the things I ate,

like ice cream, chocolate layer cake,
french fries, pizza with extra cheese
and sausage — oh, the calories
I craved and counted for the sake

of slender love without regret.
The sweet things never stayed in touch
long enough to inspire much:
who wants a serious chubbette?

The surest weight loss plan I found
was hepatitis. True, I felt
like leftovers, but I looked svelte,
and then I gained back every pound.

Again my appetite got small,
but this diet was not for choosing,
a nightmare of continued losing,
until at last I lost it all.

Epitaph for an Attendant

You saw me demonstrate the mask
and seatbelt buckle on that flight
to California. You were right:
I was, but did you have to ask?

Our training is to be polite,
not genuine. My troubled story
turned out to be respiratory,
a breathlessness not due to height.

Sick leave, then reassignment sounded
fine as I climbed to health again,
but when I tried to board the plane,
the friendly skyboys had me grounded.

I sued the airline to recover
a second time for groundless firing.
Who thinks at my age of retiring?
But their defense knew how to hover

while my condition sharply dipped
and went into its final dive.
Before a verdict could arrive
to pull me out, my wings were clipped.

Epitaph for a Barfly

Nursing a White Russian the way
I did is a fine art, like tipping,
hours on end of patient sipping,
down at the Terminal Cafe.

Blessed with a long attention span,
I dropped what dollars I could scrounge
leisurely in the cocktail lounge,
and waited for that special man,

alas, in vain. But what a place!
Done in a sort of tin-foil Deco,
with moonlit landscapes by El Greco,
it wore a lined and kindly face.

Exhausted from a day of shopping,
you could collapse, put up your feet,
and maybe have a bite to eat:
that joint was never close to hopping.

Around Miss Teena's stool there stood
the three original Teenettes,
who traded dish for cigarettes,
and swore eternal sisterhood.

Likewise disdaining fact for fable,
we dreamed of being filthy rich.
And once this macho man named Mitch
asked me to join him at his table.

Well, in two seconds I got frantic,
but my new escort pulled a switch
and acted like a tacky bitch!
Ah me, incurably romantic.

If real life had a nasty sting
and crackled with unfriendly powers,
at least the ambience was ours,
to last a lifetime's lingering.

Epitaph for an Activist

A pink triangle activist,
I lived the liberation movement
and fought for social self-improvement,
to make the languid wrist a fist.

Raised with a drawl in the Old South
that broadened some as I went on
and on up north, where I was known
in New York as a major mouth,

my tongue was sharp enough to tear
through cloudy thinking and evasion,
although for spreading sweet persuasion
I could have used a bit more care.

In younger years, I had a fix
on all gay folks as family.
It pained me to the heart to see
us squabble like a brood of chicks.

Figuring we had more to lose
as wide-ranging birds of a feather,
I tried to bind our wings together,
but a cheap shot brought down my views.

For all my talk, nobody guessed
the secret pain I kept inside,
how often I broke down and cried,
and how I left this world oppressed.

Epitaph for a Pretty Boy

Petted and called a pretty boy,
for years I had it soft as fluff,
until one day I had enough
of being just a rich man's toy.

Leaving all the designer jeans,
bikinis, skin-tight polo shirts,
mixed fruit salads, obscene desserts,
and gossip of the gilded queens,

I packed my toothbrush and a map
and hitchhiked, though I might have known
the first trucker had to be blown
before I got my midday nap.

Tired, I tried to learn the streets,
but so it went all down the line:
they knew or heard it on the vine
and rode me hard on vinyl seats.

Epitaph for a Clone

You seldom see my type alone,
in jeans and T-shirt at a bar,
trim hair and moustache, muscular,
of slight stature: in short, a clone.

No great harm in throwing this stone,
since I was born to look that way.
But if it pleases you to say
I have no soul, where is your own?

Epitaph for a Photographer

Chin down, a little to the right.
The arms look good enough to eat.
Eyes on the camera, not your feet.
Now hold it, hold that pose all night.

My ad proposed a photo session,
and some guys needed nothing more
than film and lenses to adore
themselves, while feeding my obsession.

The props and costumes got them hard,
but better were my sharp commands.
I told them where to put their hands
and got them off, and off their guard.

I got them down in black and white
and gave each one a glossy still.
Alone, I played with them at will,
developed in a different light.

My art was like a mirror trick
that fleshes out a fantasy
and gives you what you want to be,
a lasting image, with a click.

Epitaph for an Ex-con

For Christ's sake, let me out of here!
What did I do to get the can
from some disease the fags began?
And who the fuck you calling queer?

That time they framed me, and I served
without parole, I got my rocks
off with a pansy who liked jocks
and gave him just what he deserved

right up the butt, but kept my cool.
When I got out, I needed space
from Sheila, so I shared a place
with my best buddy from high school.

The jobs they give ex-cons are shit,
so why go looking? Unemployed,
I drank all day to fill the void,
until by newstime I was lit.

When Bart got home, we popped another
and worked our way to higher ground,
and yeah, we sometimes fooled around,
and now I miss him like a brother.

Epitaph for an Athlete

A high school hero, I was mobbed
as gunshot marked the final score,
and carried through the endzone for
the last-ditch touchdown pass I lobbed.

Back in those days, handsome as sin,
at six-foot-two, a dancing bear,
with chiseled features, thick, blond hair,
and a wide, razzle-dazzle grin,

a healthy, hearty specimen
in tip-top shape, I got my thrills
from long hard-hitting practice drills,
the sweat and blood and weight of men.

I lived your jockstrap fantasy,
the wet towels in the locker room,
and ass grabbing, the "crack of doom,"
all in good fun, except for me.

The chicks I dated for my image
were dumb cheerleader types who drank.
Their panties tore at the first yank,
hot to trot for a back-seat scrimmage.

My prowess landed more than praise
as college scouts came at a clip
to offer me full scholarship
for reruns of my winning plays.

Needless to say, I made the coach
quite happy on the football field,
but not when the school rag revealed
my intramural team approach.

That blew my chances as a pro,
it turned out, in the next year's draft.
First time ever, I got the shaft,
and had to think which way to go.

I figured to do well in sales,
but business-minded I was not.
My body quickly went to pot,
out of training, and broke the scales.

I drifted then from job to job,
but basically the game was over.
The stud who started out in clover
ended as a pathetic slob.

Epitaph for an Impressionist

My first appearance on the stage,
wearing a nylon wig and dress,
was not a radiant success,
if dead silence is any gauge.

Returning to the photographs
and records of my favorite star,
I learned her torch songs bar by bar
and played her slinky walk for laughs.

Engagements came in steadily
and glowing comments got around.
One night I nearly hit the ground,
when front and center, there sat she.

To my surprise, she loved the show
and led a warm standing ovation.
She helped with my pronunciation,
copied arrangements, let me know

how to get billed and introduced,
and how to look discreetly padded.
With genuine good wishes added,
she gave my act a giant boost.

She went through all her trunks as well
and filled a cab with hand-me-downs,
a fortune in designer gowns,
and sent it to my cheap hotel.

Then, while I played the Rumpus Room,
an unamused impressionee
sued in court, with publicity,
and ticket sales began to zoom.

My one-man show went on the road
and filled prestigious concert halls.
I out-belted the siren calls
of Broadway, and took up abode.

For four decades of loud acclaim,
I owe the ladies everything.
A skinny sailor who could sing
whisked on their skirts to lasting fame.

Epitaph for a Wonk

Fat lips, a nose that you could honk,
thick, horn-rimmed glasses, and a case
of zits they nicknamed "pizza face"
helped isolate me as a wonk

in high school, where I talked to girls
about a nifty theorem,
but really was afraid of them,
their teasing laughter and their curls.

Dating was of no interest.
The dumb ones liked to put me down
in public as a straight-A clown.
But seeing other boys undressed

after gym in the shower stalls,
wet and steaming, gave me a boner.
Embarrassed, I remained a loner,
hurrying through the crowded halls.

Then at state college, though I won
high honors, private life was drab.
I hung out mostly at the lab,
where I could have my type of fun.

Like once as I began to titrate
a common pentane, shot by shot,
I jerked the cock too fast and got
the formula for amyl nitrate.

I made a gallon jug that night,
and sold it by the ounce, and made
new friends who took it out in trade:
for once, the chemistry was right.

Epitaph for a Veteran

Too straight and Uncle Tom to dodge
my military obligation,
I sweated buckets on location,
in jungle boots and camouflage,

with poor white trash and racist kooks,
doing our bit for Vietnam.
And there it hit me like a bomb:
in some ways, I was like the gooks.

I counted backward through my tour
from day three hundred sixty-five.
My only hope was to survive
as days and dying friends got fewer.

With caution and some homegrown grass,
I helped relieve the tedium
of life behind the lines for some,
and traded for a weekend pass

by servicing the servicemen
who made destruction their career.
I laid my ambush from the rear,
but felt defeated even then.

By sheer luck and a low profile,
I just avoided getting shot,
but this short-timer plain forgot
how love can slay you with a smile.

Epitaph for a Homebody

Too mousey and inhibited
to cut a figure on the circuit,
no matter how I tried to work it,
I mostly stayed at home and read

the classics, all in paperback:
Thackeray, Tolstoy, Scott, and Dickens.
I liked a plot that boils and thickens,
and characters who stay on track.

For all their fascinating strife,
their chance collisions, and their doubt,
real people take the roundabout
and never come to grips with Life.

I found a few, though, who could share
my passion, as it were, by proxy,
outside the homo-orthodoxy
that pumps itself full of hot air.

When those few friends had passed away
and left me high and dry with grief,
it almost came as some relief
to know that I was on my way.

Epitaph for a Party Giver

My special parties were events,
the pulse of the community,
two thousand bodies breaking free:
the energy was so intense!

If you made tracks like Fred Astaire,
or twirled like Ginger, or just moved
your shoulders to the songs you loved,
if you liked dancing, you were there.

My mailing list of first-night names
eased out a new club called The Clutch,
about which you have heard so much,
and Sunday tea dance at Small Claims,

for which I earned a round of praise
from all the guests I urged to stay,
but not much green stuff, sad to say:
I lost my shirt promoting gays.

An owner promises the moon,
a "gold card," and a cut like his,
but when you bill for services,
he whistles for the nearest goon.

By now, my friends have ceased to roam
and altered their priorities
to fewer drugs, more wine and cheese,
dinner and quiet nights at home.

A younger generation holds
the dance floor now, the Grab Bar crowd,
first job, strange haircuts, cute and loud,
making the scene as it unfolds.

I wish them well, and from the dead,
a word of wisdom for the living:
the good you keep you get from giving —
the real party is in your head.